Fun Festivals

Diana Noonan

Contents

Festivals	2
Cheese-rolling Festival	4
Tomato Festival	6
Mud Festival	8
Snow Festival	10
Moomba Festival	12
Festival of Colour	14
Twins Festival	16
Groundhog Day Festival	18
Carabao Festival	20
Best Festival	22
Glossary	24

Festivals

People love **festivals**.
They are great fun.

Festivals are held all over the world.
Let's go and check them out!

Cheese-rolling Festival

This is a cheese-rolling festival.
People go to win a block of cheese.

Festival Facts
Where: **England**
When: **May**

A big, round cheese is rolled down a hill. Then, people race after it. The first person to the bottom of the hill wins.

Tomato Festival

This is the Tomato Festival.
People go just
to throw tomatoes.

Festival Facts
Where: **Spain**
When: **August**

They throw tomatoes at each other.
The Tomato Festival is a big food fight!

Mud Festival

This is the Mud Festival. People throw mud at each other. The mud is good for their skin.

Festival Facts
Where: **South Korea**
When: **July**

YUCK!

People play in mud pools. People roll in mud pits. Two million muddy people take part.

Snow Festival

Festival Facts
Where: **Japan**
When: **February**

This is a snow festival. People try to make the best snow and ice **sculptures**.

People from around the world come to see the sculptures. Some sculptures are bigger than houses!

Moomba Festival

This is the Moomba Festival.
People go to have fun
with friends and family.

Festival Facts
Where: **Australia**
When: **March**

Some people dress up and jump into the river.
They get very wet!

Festival of Colour

This is the Festival of Colour.
Winter is over and it is time to have fun.

Festival Facts
Where: **North India**
When: **February or March**

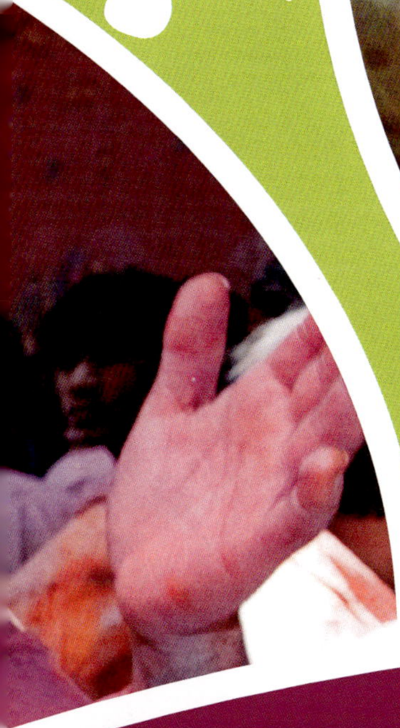

People throw coloured powder and water
at each other. The colours mean that spring is here.

Twins Festival

This is the twins festival. At this festival, people think twins are good luck.

Festival Facts
Where: **China**
When: **October**

Twins from all over the world take part.
They sing and dance and have fun.

Groundhog Day Festival

This is the Groundhog Day Festival.
People go to find out if spring will come soon.
A **groundhog** is used for this!

Festival Facts
Where: **United States of America**
When: **February**

The groundhog comes out of its home. If it sees its shadow, this means there will be six more weeks of winter. But if the day is cloudy, the groundhog will not see its shadow. This means spring will come soon.

Carabao Festival

This is the **Carabao** Festival.
It is held for farmers.

Festival Facts
Where: **Philippines**
When: **May**

Carabao work on farms. But on festival day, they have a day off. They get to walk down the streets!

Best Festival

Festivals are great fun. Think about the festivals in this book.
Which festival do you like best?

Glossary

carabao a strong animal that works in fields

festivals special events that people go to

groundhog a kind of ground squirrel

sculptures artworks made from things like snow, ice, stone or metal